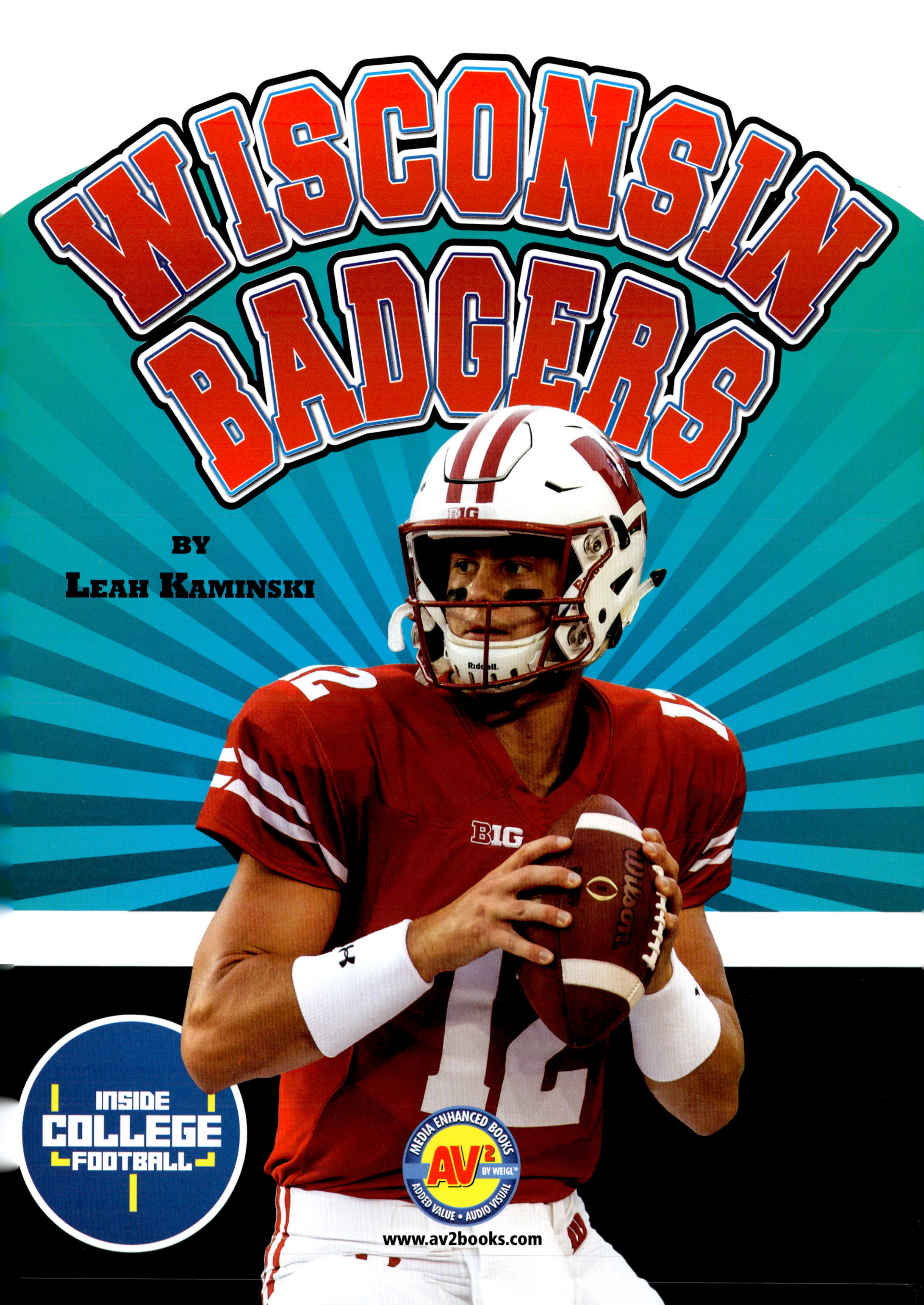

WISCONSIN BADGERS
BY
LEAH KAMINSKI
INSIDE
COLLEGE
FOOTBALL
MEDIA ENHANCED BOOKS
AV2
BY WEIGL
ADDED VALUE • AUDIO VISUAL
www.av2books.com

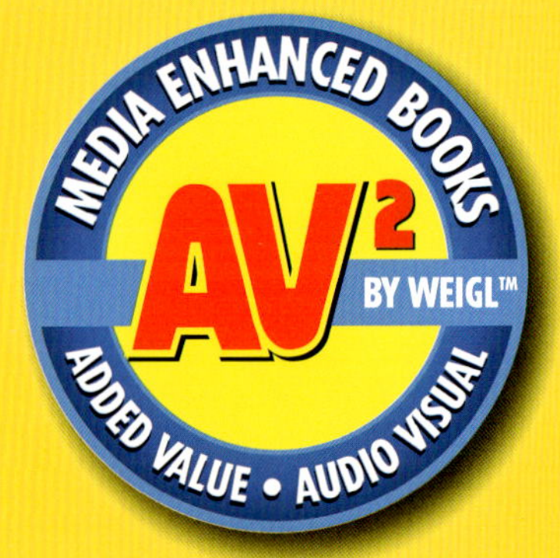

Go to **www.av2books.com,** and enter this book's unique code.

BOOK CODE

AVW22642

AV² by Weigl brings you media enhanced books that support active learning.

AV² provides enriched content that supplements and complements this book. Weigl's AV² books strive to create inspired learning and engage young minds in a total learning experience.

Your AV² Media Enhanced books come alive with...

Audio
Listen to sections of the book read aloud.

Video
Watch informative video clips.

Embedded Weblinks
Gain additional information for research.

Try This!
Complete activities and hands-on experiments.

Key Words
Study vocabulary, and complete a matching word activity.

Quizzes
Test your knowledge.

Slideshow
View images and captions, and prepare a presentation.

... and much, much more!

Published by AV² by Weigl
350 5th Avenue, 59th Floor
New York, NY 10118
Website: www.av2books.com

Library of Congress Control Number: 2018968198

ISBN 978-1-7911-0071-1 (hardcover)
ISBN 978-1-7911-0072-8 (multi-user eBook)
ISBN 978-1-7911-0074-2 (single-user eBook)

Printed in Guangzhou, China
1 2 3 4 5 6 7 8 9 0 23 22 21 20 19

042019
102318

Project Coordinator: Jared Siemens Designer: Terry Paulhus

The publisher acknowledges Alamy, Getty Images, and Newscom, and Wikimedia Commons as its primary image suppliers for this title.

Wisconsin Badgers

CONTENTS

Introduction

The Wisconsin Badgers football team are part of the Big Ten athletic conference and have won 14 Big Ten titles. The Badgers have won more than 700 games. The team has had about 26 players picked as first-team **All-Americans,** half of them in the past 20 years. About 31 former Badgers are currently signed to National Football League (NFL) teams. The Badgers have had 289 players **drafted** over their entire history and 16 first-round draft picks in the past 20 years.

Quarterback Jack Coan committed to attend the University of Wisconsin in 2016. He officially enrolled in January of 2017.

The Badgers appeared in five out of the first seven Big Ten championship games. In 2017, they won their fourth consecutive bowl game and had their second top-10 finish in *The Associated Press*'s college football poll. They also won a team-record 13 total games in 2017. In 2018, the Badgers had five players on the preseason All-America teams, tied for the most of any college.

Running back Corey Clement finished his three seasons at Wisconsin with 3,092 running yards and 38 touchdowns.

WISCONSIN

Stadium Camp Randall Stadium

Division Big Ten West

Head Coach Paul Chryst

Location Madison, Wisconsin

National Championships 0

Nicknames Badgers

9
Big Ten Championship Wins

45
Wins from 2014 to 2017

10
Shutouts since 2000

127
Seasons Played

History

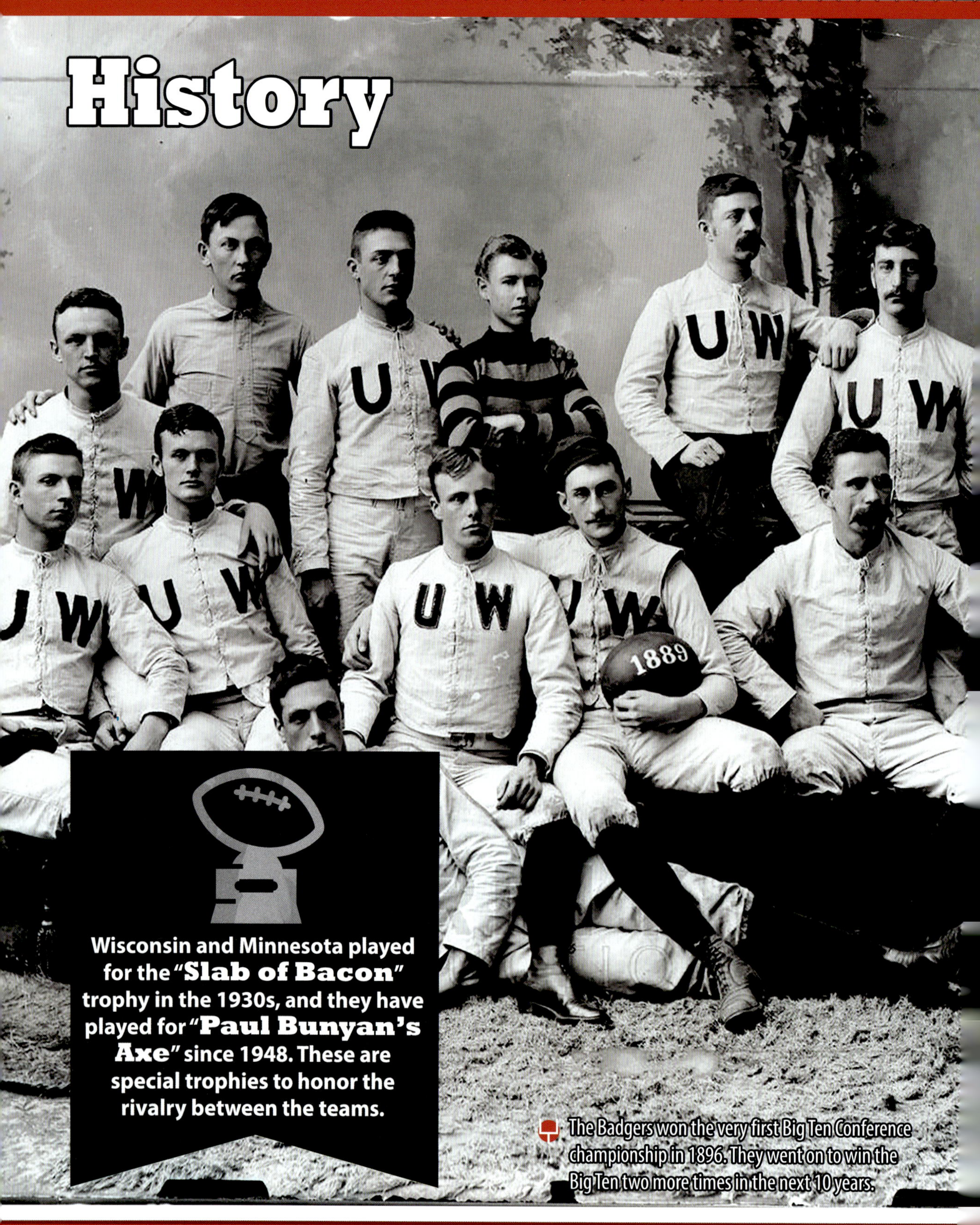

Wisconsin and Minnesota played for the "**Slab of Bacon**" trophy in the 1930s, and they have played for "**Paul Bunyan's Axe**" since 1948. These are special trophies to honor the rivalry between the teams.

The Badgers won the very first Big Ten Conference championship in 1896. They went on to win the Big Ten two more times in the next 10 years.

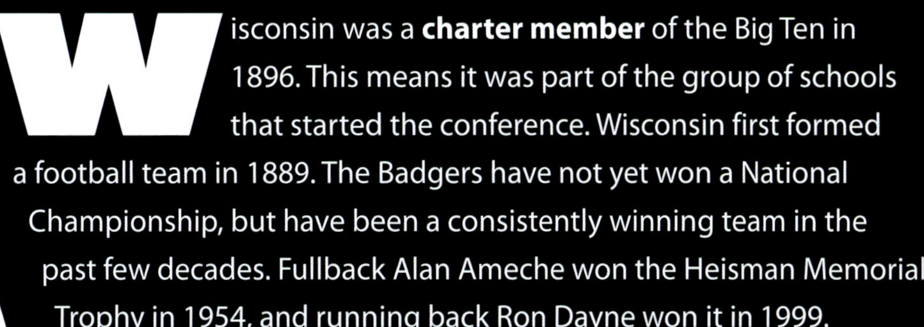

Wisconsin was a **charter member** of the Big Ten in 1896. This means it was part of the group of schools that started the conference. Wisconsin first formed a football team in 1889. The Badgers have not yet won a National Championship, but have been a consistently winning team in the past few decades. Fullback Alan Ameche won the Heisman Memorial Trophy in 1954, and running back Ron Dayne won it in 1999.

The Badgers and their fans enjoy many traditions. The University of Wisconsin Marching Band, which was founded in 1885, leads a post-game celebration after both wins and losses during what is called the "Fifth Quarter." They play traditional favorites and lead audience participation activities. The "Bud Song" has been played at every game since 1978. "Jump Around" has been played between the third and fourth quarters since 1998. When the Badgers win a game, members of the band turn their hats around and wear them backwards.

The Badgers have several long-running rivalries, including the "Border Battle" against Minnesota. This is the most-played rivalry in Division I football. It has been played almost continuously since 1890. Wisconsin has a win streak of 14 and an overall winning record in the series.

Australian kicker Pat O'Dea was nicknamed "the Kangaroo Kicker." According to Wisconsin legend, O'Dea once drop-kicked a 62-yard field goal to beat Northwestern during a blizzard in 1898.

The Stadium

Before Camp Randall Stadium was built, the football and baseball teams played on an all-purpose athletic field in the same spot, which had only rickety wooden bleachers for spectators.

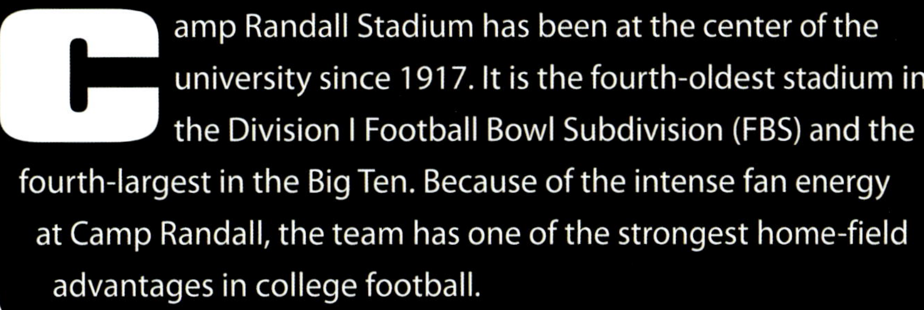

Camp Randall Stadium has been at the center of the university since 1917. It is the fourth-oldest stadium in the Division I Football Bowl Subdivision (FBS) and the fourth-largest in the Big Ten. Because of the intense fan energy at Camp Randall, the team has one of the strongest home-field advantages in college football.

The stadium was named after Wisconsin's first wartime governor, Alexander W. Randall. The land was originally used to train Wisconsin troops. The first football game was played there in 1895, and the stadium broke ground in 1915. The first game in the new stadium was against Minnesota in 1917. During World War I (1914–1918) and World War II (1939–1945), troops were again stationed there for training.

The stadium's most recent **renovation** cost $109.5 million and was completed between 2001 and 2005. It raised the seating capacity to 80,321. The stadium's record attendance was in 2004. An average of 82,368 fans attended games that season. The largest single crowd was 83,184 in 2005. The stadium has been top 16 in the United States in attendance since 1972.

The arch at Camp Randall's entrance is a memorial to the 70,000 soldiers who were trained for Civil War combat at the training site where the stadium now stands.

Where They Play

Welcome to Camp Randall Stadium. The stands are a sea of red and white. Game-day traditions and passion for Wisconsin football bring fans and players together, here at the home of the Badgers.

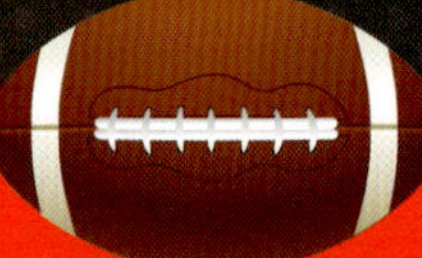

BIG TEN WEST

1. **Northwestern University**
   Evanston, Illinois
2. **Purdue University**
   West Lafayette, Indiana
3. **University of Illinois**
   Urbana-Champaign, Illinois
4. **University of Iowa**
   Iowa City, Iowa
5. **University of Minnesota**
   Minneapolis, Minnesota
6. **University of Nebraska**
   Lincoln, Nebraska
7. ★ **University of Wisconsin**
   Madison, Wisconsin

Arena
Camp Randall Stadium

Location
Madison, Wisconsin

Broke Ground
1915

Completed
1917

Surface
Artificial Turf

Features
- High-definition scoreboard in the stadium measures 4,271 square feet
- Life-size sculptures of coach Barry Alvarez and director of athletics Pat Richter in front of Gate 1
- Badger Alley, a concourse inside the stadium, features a timeline of Camp Randall and Badgers football

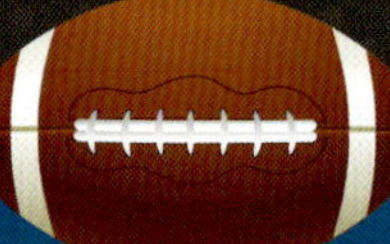

BIG TEN EAST

1. **Indiana University**
   Bloomington, Indiana
2. **Michigan State University**
   East Lansing, Michigan
3. **Ohio State University**
   Columbus, Ohio
4. **Pennsylvania State University**
   State College, Pennsylvania
5. **Rutgers University–New Brunswick**
   New Brunswick–Piscataway, New Jersey
6. **University of Maryland**
   College Park, Maryland
7. **University of Michigan**
   Ann Arbor, Michigan

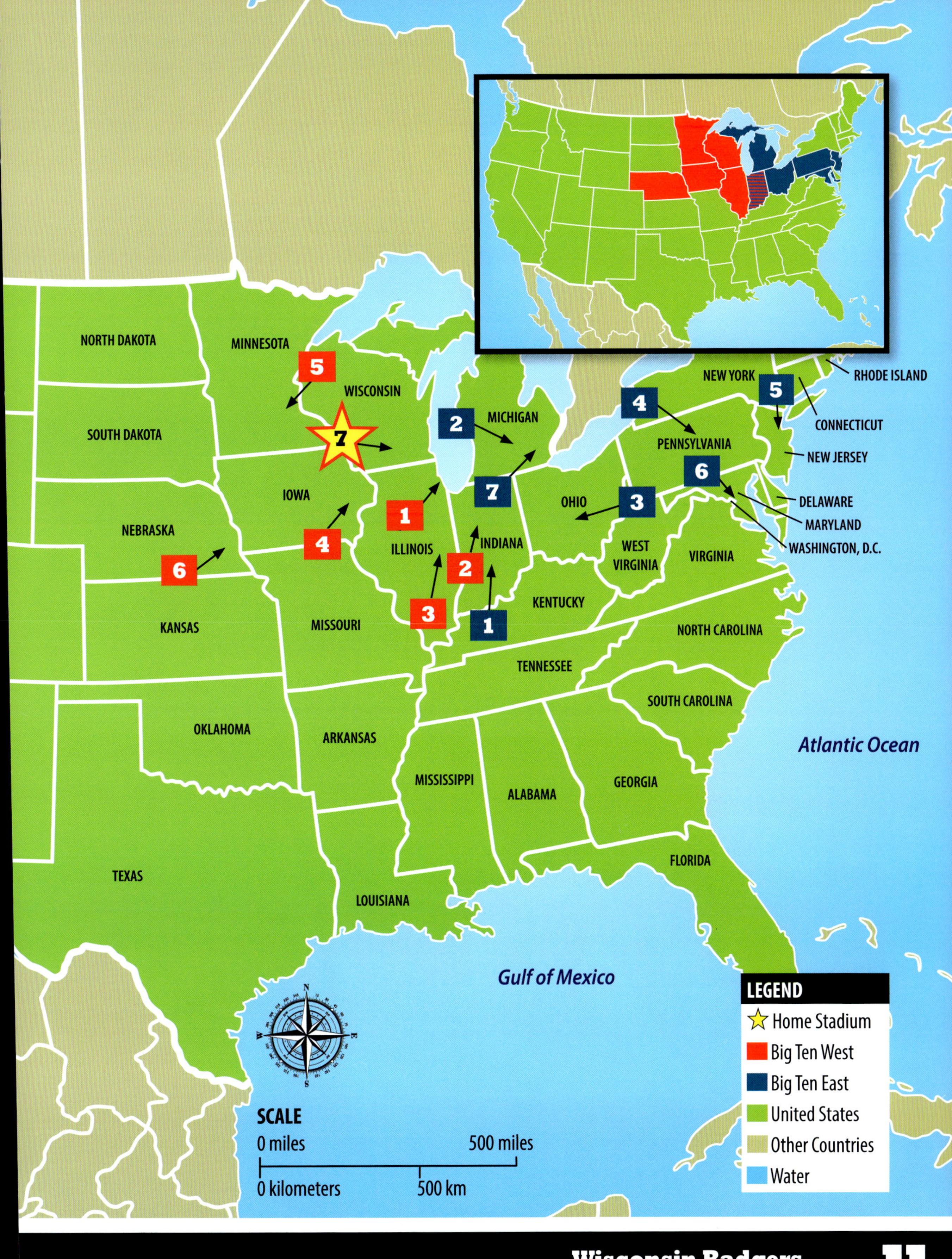

NORTH DAKOTA
MINNESOTA
WISCONSIN
SOUTH DAKOTA
MICHIGAN
NEW YORK
RHODE ISLAND
CONNECTICUT
PENNSYLVANIA
NEW JERSEY
IOWA
NEBRASKA
OHIO
DELAWARE
MARYLAND
WASHINGTON, D.C.
ILLINOIS
INDIANA
WEST VIRGINIA
VIRGINIA
KANSAS
MISSOURI
KENTUCKY
NORTH CAROLINA
TENNESSEE
SOUTH CAROLINA
OKLAHOMA
ARKANSAS
Atlantic Ocean
MISSISSIPPI
ALABAMA
GEORGIA
TEXAS
FLORIDA
LOUISIANA
Gulf of Mexico
LEGEND
Home Stadium
Big Ten West
Big Ten East
United States
Other Countries
Water
SCALE
0 miles
500 miles
0 kilometers
500 km

The Uniforms

The Wisconsin 2012 Rose Bowl **helmets** had a subtle pattern of **red-on-red roses** inside the numbers.

Former Wisconsin running back Dare Ogunbowale rushed for more than 1,500 yards in a Badgers uniform from 2013 to 2016.

The University of Wisconsin's colors are cardinal red and white. For many years, the team's uniforms have stayed the same. They wear red jerseys at home and white jerseys on the road, with white pants and a white helmet. Sometimes they wear red pants on the road for special games, like the 2012 Rose Bowl.

HOME

Since 1970, the Badgers have almost always worn a helmet with a red "W" over a white background. Their uniforms have had a **logo** called the "Motion W" since head coach Barry Alvarez introduced it in the 1990s. This replaced the block "W."

AWAY

In the 2013 season, the team introduced 20 different possible uniform combinations, though not all were worn. The uniforms have had arrows on them since 2017. The arrows are meant to reflect the Wisconsin state motto, which is "Forward."

There are three other teams in the Big Ten Conference whose colors are red and white. The addition of the "Forever Forward" arrows in 2017 was one way of setting the Badgers' uniforms apart.

Student Athletes

Since 1990, **19** walk-on Badgers have gone on to play in the **NFL**.

Offensive lineman Jon Dietzen helped the Badgers finish second in the Big Ten in rushing offense and third in total offense in 2017 before having off-season surgery to repair hip injuries.

Being a college student athlete is hard work. Student athletes have to perform well on the football field and in the classroom. Wisconsin student athletes are required to meet a minimum grade point average. Wisconsin student athletes benefit from the Stephen M. Bennett Student-Athlete Performance Center. The center provides academic support, fitness training, and sports medicine care.

Many student athletes are given athletic scholarships. An athletic scholarship is a financial aid agreement between the athlete and their college or university. Athletes who do not receive a scholarship can be "walk-on" members of the team. This means they are on the team without financial aid. Walk-on players have been a crucial part of the team since Barry Alvarez coached the Badgers in the 1990s. The team often gives scholarships to walk-on players in their third and fourth years. Wisconsin typically awards the maximum number of athletic scholarships allowed, which is 85.

Running back Garrett Groshek turned down scholarship offers at other schools to play football for the Badgers. After one season as a walk-on player, Groshek was awarded a full scholarship for his remaining time at Wisconsin.

Bowl Games

The Badgers have participated in a season-ending bowl game for **18** consecutive seasons.

Wisconsin scored their only two touchdowns of the 2013 Rose Bowl in the second quarter. The Badgers were defeated 14–20 by the Stanford Cardinal.

Bowl Games are a unique sports tradition in college football. In the beginning of college football, there was no true **postseason**. Today, a variety of postseason bowl games are played. Bowl games give teams the opportunity to continue striving for recognition and victory after the end of regular play. There are currently 40 bowl games played in various combinations each year. These games are chosen with input from teams, sponsors, and the College Football Playoff Selection Committee. The game matchups are announced in December.

The Badgers have a 16–14 bowl record. Former head coach Barry Alvarez has the team's best bowl record so far, at 8–3. The Badgers have played in nine Rose Bowls, including a loss to the University of Southern California (USC) in 1963. This game was one of the greatest bowl games ever. The 79 combined points were a Rose Bowl record for 28 years.

The Badgers defeated the University of Miami in the Pinstripe Bowl in 2018. This was their fifth consecutive bowl win. Only three other teams in the nation have had such a long winning streak.

Wisconsin's 15 bowl game wins include three Rose Bowl victories.

The Coaches

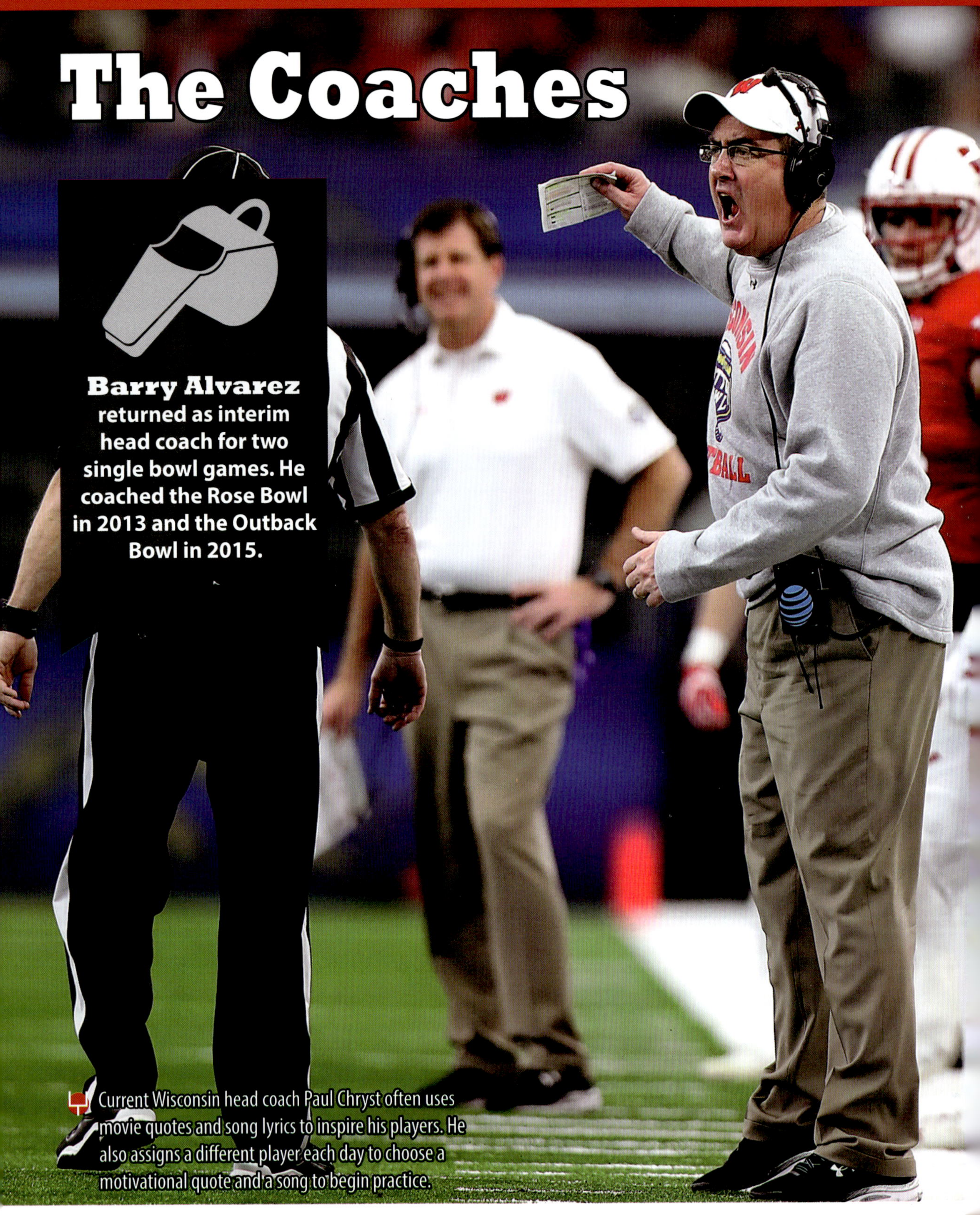

Barry Alvarez returned as interim head coach for two single bowl games. He coached the Rose Bowl in 2013 and the Outback Bowl in 2015.

Current Wisconsin head coach Paul Chryst often uses movie quotes and song lyrics to inspire his players. He also assigns a different player each day to choose a motivational quote and a song to begin practice.

The Badgers have had 29 coaches since the team's inception. Some Badgers coaches have won as many as 119 games, while others won none at all. Barry Alvarez won the most, and Alvin Kletsch, the Badger's first coach in 1889, won the least. Of those coaches, four are members of the College Football **Hall of Fame** and three have won Big Ten Coach of the Year honors.

IVY WILLIAMSON Ivy Williamson's 1949 team finished 5–3–1 to begin six consecutive winning seasons. His 1951 team set several school records that still stand for scoring defense, total defense, and rushing defense. In 1952, Wisconsin won its first Big Ten title since 1912 and appeared in its first-ever Rose Bowl. Williamson then worked as the Badgers' athletic director from 1955 to 1969.

BARRY ALVAREZ It is said that Barry Alvarez brought the Badgers "from red ink to roses" because he was such a winning coach. Alvarez was National Coach of the Year in 1993. He was Big Ten Coach of the Year in 1993 and 1998. He is now Wisconsin's director of athletics. He is a member of the College Football Hall of Fame.

PAUL CHRYST Paul Chryst is a Madison native and former quarterback for the Badgers. He has a 0.829 win percentage since he started in 2014, the fifth-best in college football. Every season he has coached at Wisconsin has been a winning season. Chryst has won two consecutive Big Ten Coach of the Year awards.

The Mascot

Bucky appears at every home football game, as well as other athletic events, parades, local festivals, and even weddings and other ceremonies connected to the university.

The Badgers took their name from Wisconsin's nickname, "the Badger State." The badger has been the official University of Wisconsin mascot since the first season of intercollegiate football in 1889. The original live badger mascot was difficult to control and would often escape. It was retired to the Madison Henry Vilas Zoo.

The current mascot, Bucky, was first drawn in 1940. A student began dressing as Bucky by wearing a papier-mâché badger head on the sidelines. At first, he went by names such as Benny, Bernie, and Bouncey. The winner of a 1949 naming contest was Buckingham U. Badger, or Bucky. Bucky Badger wears a red-and-white letter sweater and red athletic shoes. During games, Bucky interacts with fans, dances, and does push-ups to match the score.

The tryouts for students who want to play Bucky Badger include doing as many push-ups as possible, performing skits with random props, and an interview with the Athletic Department.

Legends of the Past

For many players, their time with the Badgers is the start of a promising football career. These are some of the best-known football players to play for the University of Wisconsin.

Ron Dayne

Ron Dayne won the Heisman Trophy in 1999. That same year, he was also a consensus All-American and the Big Ten MVP. He rushed more than 200 yards in five different games his senior year. He still holds the National Collegiate Athletic Association (NCAA) career record of 6,397 rushing yards. Dayne was MVP of the 1999 and 2000 Rose Bowls. He is a member of the College Football Hall of Fame and the Rose Bowl Hall of Fame. Dayne was drafted 11th overall by the New York Giants in 2000, and he went to the **Super Bowl** with them that year. Dayne also played for the Denver Broncos and the Houston Texans before retiring in 2007.

Position: Running Back
Seasons: 1996–1999 (Wisconsin Badgers), 2000–2004 (New York Giants), 2005 (Denver Broncos), 2006–2007 (Houston Texans)
Born: March 14, 1978, Berlin, Virginia

Joe Thomas

As a Badger, Joe Thomas was a two-time first-team All-American. He was named a National Scholar-Athlete by the National Football Foundation and was an *ESPN The Magazine* second-team Academic All-American in 2006. Thomas started 39 games during his college career. The Cleveland Browns drafted him third overall in 2007, and he retired in 2017. One of the greatest linemen of all time, he was invited to the **Pro Bowl** each of his 10 seasons. Thomas's 10,363 consecutive snaps played is the longest streak since counting began in 1999.

Position: Offensive Tackle
Seasons: 2005–2006 (Wisconsin Badgers), 2007–2017 (Cleveland Browns)
Born: December 4, 1984, Brookfield, Wisconsin

J.J. Watt

Defensive end J.J. Watt walked on for Wisconsin after beginning his career at Central Michigan. He was a consensus All-Big Ten and Academic All-Big Ten in 2010. He was also his team's **Most Valuable Player (MVP)** in 2010. Watt was drafted by the Houston Texans 11th overall in 2011 and still plays for them. He was a three-time NFL Defensive Player of the Year. Nicknamed "the Milkman" and "J.J. Swatt," Watt is a four-time first-team **All-Pro** and four-time Pro Bowl selection. His younger brother T.J. also played for the Badgers and now plays in the NFL.

Position: Defensive End
Seasons: 2009–2010 (Wisconsin Badgers), 2011–Present (Houston Texans)
Born: March 22, 1989, Waukesha, Wisconsin

Russell Wilson

Russell Wilson came to Wisconsin for his final college season. He spent three years with North Carolina State University in the Atlantic Coast Conference. Wilson set records for both teams, and was drafted by the Seahawks in the third round in 2012. He tied Peyton Manning's record for most passing touchdowns by an NFL rookie. Wilson led the Seahawks to their first-ever Super Bowl victory in 2013. Today, Wilson still plays for the Seahawks. He has won more games than any other NFL quarterback in their first six seasons (65). Wilson is the shortest quarterback to ever win the Super Bowl, at 5 feet 11 inches (180 centimeters) tall.

Position: Quarterback
Seasons: 2011 (Wisconsin Badgers), 2012–Present (Seattle Seahawks)
Born: November 29, 1988, Cincinnati, Ohio

All-Time Records

618
Points in a Season
The Badgers scored a season-record 618 points in 2011, the same season they won the Big Ten Championship.

3,175
Passing Yards in a Season
Quarterback Russell Wilson set the record for most passing yards in a season, with 3,175 in 2011.

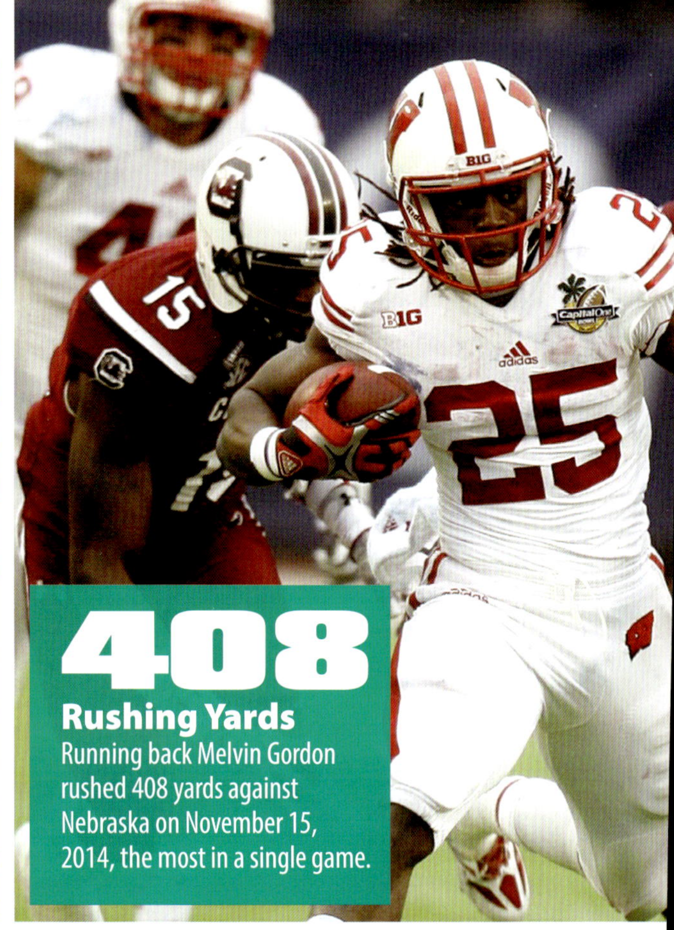

408
Rushing Yards
Running back Melvin Gordon rushed 408 yards against Nebraska on November 15, 2014, the most in a single game.

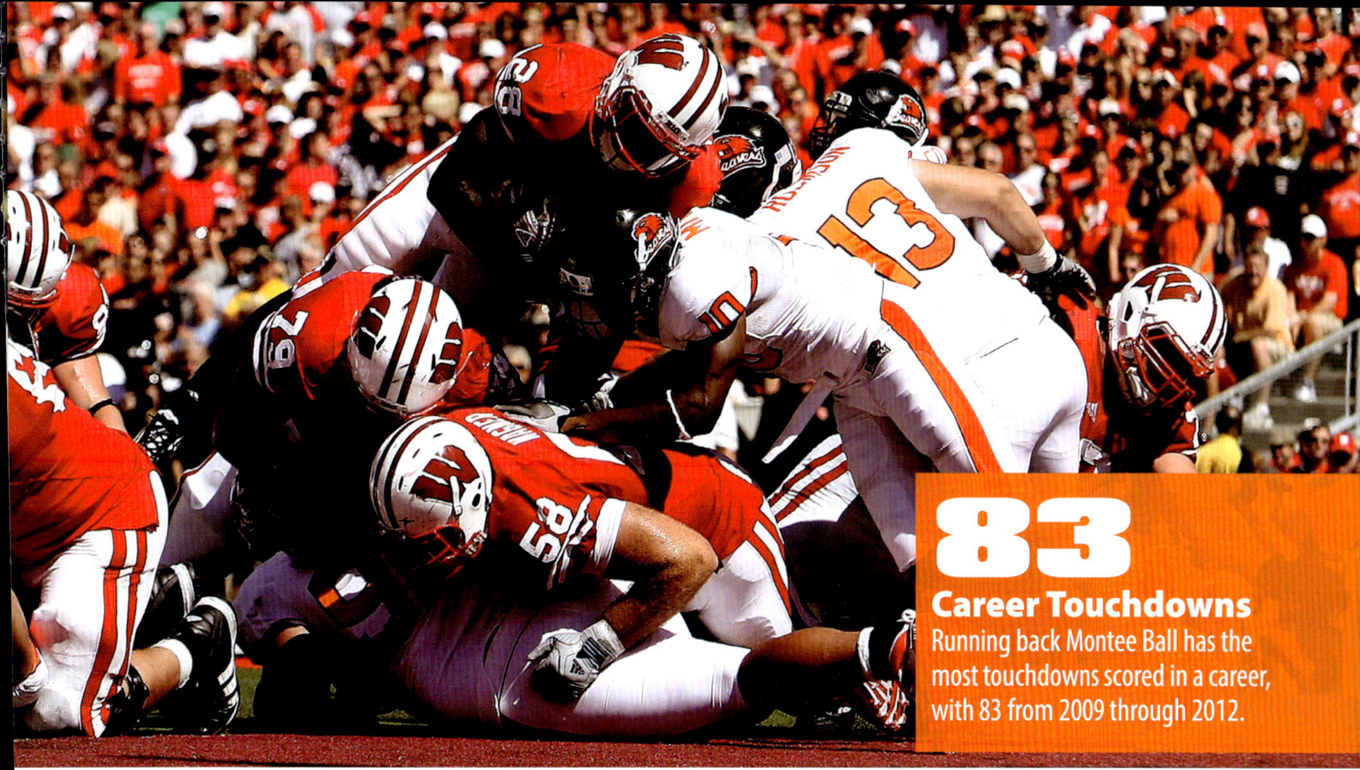

83
Career Touchdowns
Running back Montee Ball has the most touchdowns scored in a career, with 83 from 2009 through 2012.

22
Sacks
Defensive end Tom Burke holds the Wisconsin record for most quarterback sacks in a season, with 22 in the 1998 season.

Timeline

Throughout the team's history, the Wisconsin Badgers have had many memorable events that have become defining moments for the team and its fans.

On November 23, 1889, Wisconsin plays its first intercollegiate football game, losing 27–0 to the Calumet Club team of Milwaukee. The coach finishes his single-year career 0–2.

1942
After decades of losing seasons, the Badgers are ranked second in the nation after defeating number-one Ohio State 17–7. Two Badgers from that game, including Elroy "Crazylegs" Hirsch, serve in World War II (WWII) after this season.

1880 | 1900 | 1920 | 1940

1890
The first Border Battle is played in Minneapolis. The University of Minnesota wins 63–0 to begin the most-played rivalry in college football.

1896
The Badgers win the first Western Conference (Big Ten) Championship under Phil King, in a 7–1–1 season.

1917
Camp Randall Stadium is dedicated with a 10–7 Badgers homecoming victory over Minnesota.

The Future

The Badgers had some difficult seasons in the 1970s and 1980s, but they have become a very successful team in recent years. They have had more than 20 consecutive winning seasons. The Badgers have appeared in bowl games for 15 years running, a Big Ten record. This is a testament to their strength in the modern era.

1990

Barry Alvarez becomes the 27th head coach of the Badgers, ushering in a return to winning seasons and a proud modern era.

2000

The Badgers win their second consecutive Rose Bowl after defeating Stanford 17–9. They're the first team in Big Ten history to win consecutive Rose Bowls. Ron Dayne wins his second consecutive Rose Bowl MVP Award.

1960 1980 2000 2020

On January 1, 1994, the Badgers win the Rose Bowl for the first time, against the Bruins. Big Ten Offensive Player of the Year Brent Moss is MVP of the game.

1953

The Badgers play in their first-ever bowl game, losing to USC in the Rose Bowl, the only Rose Bowl appearance under coach Ivy Williamson.

2011

Wisconsin defeats Michigan State 42–39 in the inaugural Big Ten Football Championship Game. The Badgers win their second consecutive Big Ten title, the first outright since 1999.

Write a Biography

Life Story

A person's life story can be the subject of a book. This kind of book is called a biography. Biographies often describe the lives of people who have achieved great success. These people may be alive today, or they may have lived many years ago. Reading a biography can help you learn more about a great person.

Get the Facts

Use this book, and research in the library and on the internet, to find out more about your favorite player. Learn as much about him as you can. What position does he play? What are his statistics in important categories? Has he set any records? Also, be sure to write down key events in the person's life. What was his childhood like? What has he accomplished off the field? Is there anything else that makes this person special or unusual?

Use the Concept Web

A concept web is a useful research tool. Read the questions in the concept web on the following page. Answer the questions in your notebook. Your answers will help you write a biography.

Concept Web

Write a Biography

Adulthood

- Where does this individual currently reside?
- Does he have a family?

Your Opinion

- What did you learn from the books you read in your research?
- Would you suggest these books to others?
- Was anything missing from these books?

Childhood

- Where and when was this person born?
- Describe his parents, siblings, and friends.
- Did this person grow up in unusual circumstances?

Accomplishments off the Field

- What is this person's life's work?
- Has he received awards or recognition for accomplishments?
- How have this person's accomplishments served others?

Help and Obstacles

- Did this individual have a positive attitude?
- Did he receive help from others?
- Did this person have a mentor?
- Did this person face any hardships?
- If so, how were the hardships overcome?

Accomplishments on the Field

- What records does this person hold?
- What key games and plays have defined his career?
- What are his stats in categories important to his position?

Work and Preparation

- What was this person's education?
- What was his work experience?
- How does this person work?
- What is the process he uses?

Trivia Time

Take this quiz to test your knowledge of the Wisconsin Badgers. The answers are printed upside down under each question.

1 What is the name of the Badgers' stadium?

A. Camp Randall Stadium

2 What year was the Badgers' first year of football?

A. 1889

3 What is the name of the yearly Wisconsin-Minnesota game?

A. The Border Battle

4 What are Wisconsin's school colors?

A. Cardinal red and white

5 Which coach brought the team "from red ink to roses"?

A. Barry Alvarez

6 What is the name of the Badgers' mascot?

A. Bucky Badger

7 Which Wisconsin quarterback led the Seahawks to their first-ever Super Bowl Victory in 2013?

A. Russell Wilson

8 What Badger has a brother who followed him to Wisconsin and then the NFL?

A. J.J. Watt

9 What player scored the most touchdowns during his career?

A. Montee Ball

10 What's the name of the post-game celebration at Camp Randall?

A. The Fifth Quarter

Key Words

All-Americans: players, usually in high school or college, judged to be the best in each position of a sport

All-Pro: a term used to designate the best players of each position during a given season

charter member: an original or founding member of a group or organization

drafted: chosen to play professionally in the National Football League during an annual event

Hall of Fame: a group of persons judged to be outstanding in a particular sport

logo: a symbol that stands for a team or organization

Most Valuable Player (MVP): the player judged to be most valuable to his team's success

postseason: a sporting event that takes place after the end of the regular season

Pro Bowl: the annual all-star game for NFL players pitting the best players in the National Football Conference against the best players in the American Football Conference

renovation: construction that works to improve or expand an older building

Super Bowl: the NFL's annual championship game between the winning team from the National Football Conference and the winning team from the American Football Conference

Index

Log on to www.av2books.com

AV² by Weigl brings you media enhanced books that support active learning. Go to www.av2books.com, and enter the special code found on page 2 of this book. You will gain access to enriched and enhanced content that supplements and complements this book. Content includes video, audio, weblinks, quizzes, a slideshow, and activities.

AV² Online Navigation

Audio
Listen to sections of the book read aloud.

Book Pages
AV² pages directly correspond to pages in the book.

Video
Watch informative video clips.

Embedded Weblinks
Gain additional information for research.

Key Words
Study vocabulary, and complete a matching word activity.

Try This!
Complete activities and hands-on experiments.

Quizzes
Test your knowledge.

Slideshow
View images and captions, and prepare a presentation.

AV² was built to bridge the gap between print and digital. We encourage you to tell us what you like and what you want to see in the future.

Sign up to be an AV² Ambassador at www.av2books.com/ambassador.

Due to the dynamic nature of the internet, some of the URLs and activities provided as part of AV² by Weigl may have changed or ceased to exist. AV² by Weigl accepts no responsibility for any such changes. All media enhanced books are regularly monitored to update addresses and sites in a timely manner. Contact AV² by Weigl at 1-866-649-3445 or av2books@weigl.com with any questions, comments, or feedback.